ANCIENT COMMUNICATION

ANCIENT TECHNOLOGY

ANCIENT COMMUNICATION

FROM GRUNTS TO GRAFFITI

by Michael Woods

and

Mary B. Woods

RP RUNESTONE PRESS • MINNEAPOLIS

A DIVISION OF LERNER PUBLISHING GROUP

Dedicated to Natalie, David, Martha, Mark, Cathy, and Frances

Series designer: Zachary Marell
Series editors: Joelle E. Riley and Dina Drits
Line editor: Margaret J. Goldstein

Runestone Press
A division of Lerner Publishing Group
241 First Avenue North
Minneapolis, MN 55401 U.S.A.

Website address: www.lernerbooks.com

LIBRARY OF CONGRESS CATALOGING-IN-PUBLICATION DATA

Woods, Michael, 1946–
    Ancient communication: from grunts to graffiti / Michael and Mary B. Woods.
      p.   cm. — (Ancient technology)
    Includes bibliographical references and index.
    Summary: Examines ancient methods of communication in the Middle East, India, China, Egypt, Greece, Rome, and Mesoamerica.
    ISBN 0–8225–2996–3 (lib. bdg. : alk. paper)
    1. Communication—History—Juvenile literature. [1. Communication—History.] I. Woods, Michael, 1943– II. Title. III. Series.
P91.2.W59 2000
302.2'09—dcd21   99-49934

Manufactured in the United States of America
1 2 3 4 5 6 – AM – 05 04 03 02 01 00

TABLE OF CONTENTS

What do you think of when you hear the word *technology?* You probably think of something totally new. You might think of research laboratories filled with computers, powerful microscopes, and other scientific tools. But technology doesn't refer only to brand-new machines and discoveries. Technology is as old as human society.

Technology is the use of knowledge, inventions, and discoveries to make life better. The word *technology* comes from two Greek words. One, *tekhne*, means "art" or "craft." The other, *logos*, means "word" or "speech." To the ancient Greeks, *technology* meant a discussion of arts and crafts. In modern times, the word usually refers to an art or craft itself.

People use many kinds of technology. Construction is one kind of technology. Medicine and agriculture are also kinds of technology. These technologies and many others make life easier, safer, and more enjoyable. This book looks at a form of technology that helps make all other kinds of technology possible. That technology is communication.

Without communication, there would be no civilization. The word *civilization* comes from the Latin *civitas*, meaning "city." However, people must do more than build cities to be civilized. Civilizations also have governments, religions, social classes, distinct occupations, and methods for keeping records.

When the earliest humans started communicating,

they were able to settle disputes, cooperate with each other, and plan ahead. They could settle into permanent villages and live peacefully. As villages grew into cities and life became more complicated, people needed better ways of keeping records. They developed languages and wrote stories and books. Some experts think that writing was the greatest invention in history.

ANCIENT ROOTS

You've probably heard people remark, "There's nothing new under the sun!" There's much truth in the saying when we're talking about communication. People who lived thousands of years ago developed our most basic communication tools. For instance, the ancient Chinese invented a material 1,900 years ago that has never been surpassed for written communication. That material is paper.

The word *ancient*, as used in this book, refers to the period from the emergence of the first humans on earth to the fall of the Western Roman Empire in A.D. 476. The first humans lived about 2.5 million years ago.

Technology is one trait that distinguishes humans from their pre-human ancestors. The first human communication technology was simple, yet it was effective. Our early ancestors probably grunted, growled, and snarled to pass information to each other. Later, people used sharp sticks to draw images in pieces of wet clay. Those images were the first kinds of writing.

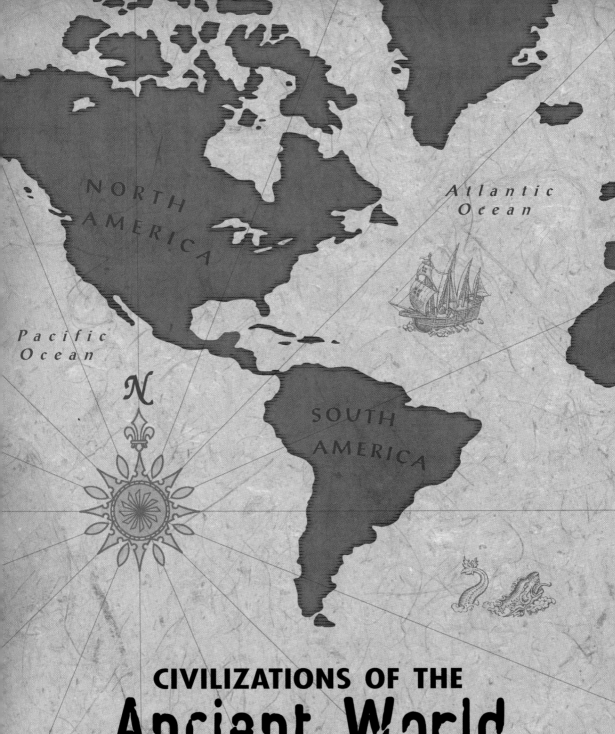

CIVILIZATIONS OF THE
Ancient World
(through A.D. 476)

EUROPE

ASIA

AFRICA

Indian
Ocean

6000 B.C.					534 B.C.	Middle East
3100 B.C.				30 B.C.		Egypt
	1766 B.C.					China
	1200 B.C.					Mesoamerica
		800 B.C.		146 B.C.		Greece
		509 B.C.		A.D. 476		Rome
		320 B.C.				India

Stone Age civilizations have flourished in
most parts of the world. These cultures began and
ended at different times in different regions.

What Is Communication?

To communicate is to share news, ideas, feelings, and images with other people. Communication involves more than just speaking, writing, and reading, however. It includes art, music, dance, signals, and other nonverbal forms of sharing information, as well as equipment used in sharing information. Paper, pens, ink, paintbrushes, musical instruments, and books are all forms of communication technology.

Ancient people developed new communication technology by trial and error. Sometimes they copied communication technology invented in other countries and added their own new touches. For instance, the ancient Phoenicians developed the first alphabet in the Western world. The Greeks, Etruscans, and Romans all added their own changes and improvements to the alphabet.

The ancient Romans spread their communication technology through war. As they conquered other groups, they spread the Latin language throughout Europe. That's why so many modern languages, including English, contain Latin words.

A Lot with a Little

Ancient people didn't have television, printing presses, or the Internet—yet they communicated very well. The ancient Greeks and Romans wrote stories, poems, and plays. Many of these writings are classics—some of the best literature ever created—and modern people still study them. Ancient writers also produced one of the world's most famous books—the Bible. Some ancient civilizations even developed postal systems. Read on and discover how ancient people created these and many other communication technologies—many of them still used.

THE STONE AGE

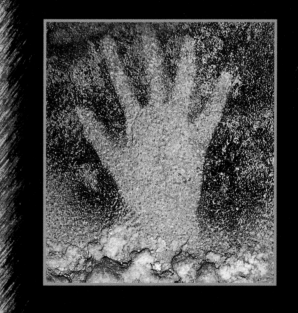

Cave painting of human handprints and
deer, from Patagonia, South America

The first humans lived in Africa about 2.5
million years ago. They were hunters and
gatherers—they hunted game, caught fish,
and gathered wild plants for food. Because these first humans used many tools made
of stone, we call the first period of human history the Stone Age.

The earliest humans lived and traveled in
small family groups. They probably communicated with utterances—grunts and growls—long
before they made specific sounds to stand for
specific objects or ideas. They probably relied
on gestures, their sense of smell, and other
methods of sending and receiving information.
They probably used smoke signals, drumbeats,
and fires to send messages over long distances.

Although primitive, such communication
technology was probably quite effective. Remember, early humans lived in small groups
and knew each other very, very well. Contact
with strangers was probably rare. In such a

tight-knit group, it was easy to guess what other people wanted and meant.

THE TALKING ANIMAL

Animals communicate with barks, growls, squawks, hisses, whistles, meows, purrs, yelps, moos, baas, whinnies, and other utterances. Many of these sounds are actually warnings. For instance, a songbird's cry in spring may sound beautiful, but experts believe the bird's song really means: "Stay out of my territory!"

Although some animal sounds carry meaning, humans are the only animals who can speak and carry on conversations. Many scientists believe that our ancestors officially became "human" when they developed the ability to speak. Spoken language gave people power to pass on information, share ideas, organize activities, and cooperate with others on projects that could not be done by one person alone. With speech, people could discuss the past and plan for the future. Spoken language led to changes in human behavior and to advancements in society, art, religion, and tools.

The first humans could not speak. Their mouths and throats were suited mainly for chewing, swallowing, and breathing. Their larynxes (voice boxes) were set too high in their throats for speech, and their mouths were too long.

About one million years ago, however, humans began changing. Their larynxes moved lower. Their skulls changed shape, producing a shorter mouth. Most important, their brains began to enlarge. Most of this growth occurred in areas of the brain needed for speech.

Many scientists believe that between 150,000 and 200,000 years ago, our ancestors had bodies ready for modern speech. Other scientists think that speech developed only about 40,000 years ago, when people began making tools, living in groups, and burying their dead. These scientists think that the ability to speak went hand in hand with these other advancements in human society.

"LOOK, FATHER! BULLS!"

One morning in 1879, Don Marcellino de Sautuola took his young daughter, Maria, to explore a cave near their home in Altamira in northern Spain. With light from an oil lamp, Don Marcellino studied animal bones and stone tools on the cave floor. An amateur archaeologist (a scientist who studies the remains of past cultures), he knew that people had used the cave thousands of years earlier. After a while, Maria got tired. She found a comfortable stone ledge and lay down, gazing at the cave walls in the flickering lamplight.

"Bulls!" Maria suddenly cried out. "Look, Father! There they are!" Don Marcellino quickly ran to his daughter. She was pointing at the cave walls. They were covered with colored drawings of buffalo, antelope, and other animals that had not lived in Spain for thousands of years.

Maria had discovered Stone Age cave paintings. The Altamira caves quickly became world famous. Soon many more cave paintings were discovered in other parts of the world.

Archaeologists think that people began making cave paintings and other artwork about 50,000 years ago. Some of the oldest known Stone Age paintings, created about 32,000 years ago, were made on the wall of a cave near Grotte Chauvet in southern France. Another cave, near the French town of Vallon-Pont-d'Arc, contains more than three hundred paintings made 20,000 years ago. Many cave

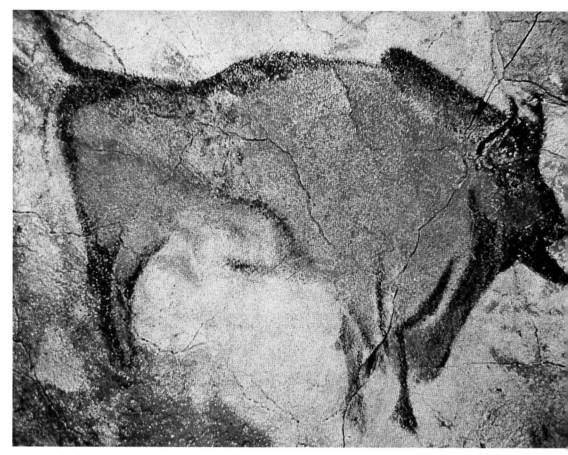

Twelve-thousand-year-old painting of a bull from the Altamira caves in Spain

paintings include beautiful and lifelike images of bears, lions, mammoths, horses, woolly rhinoceroses, and wild cats. Some painters took advantage of natural bumps and grooves on cave walls to represent parts of animals' bodies.

In addition to painting on cave walls, Stone Age people carved images of animals from ivory and stone. They carved designs on animal bones and on the teeth of woolly mammoths. One 30,000-year-old bone contains carvings that seem to record the phases of the moon—the changing appearance of the moon in the sky each night.

Why are cave paintings and other artworks important? These works show us how Stone Age people started to communicate with symbols, not just with sounds and actions. The earliest humans probably screamed, gestured, smiled, cried, punched, and shoved to get their messages across. This kind of communication lasted only a moment, then disappeared.

But artwork made communication more permanent. With a painting or drawing, people could relay the same message time and again. Art encouraged people to remember experiences, think about them, and record them for others to understand. By creating artwork, our ancestors were becoming more intelligent—more human.

How Do We Know?

How old are the cave paintings? Archaeologists have several ways of finding out. In some cases, the pictures show animals that are extinct. Suppose a cave painting shows a woolly rhinoceros. From studying fossils and other evidence, scientists know when woolly rhinoceroses became extinct. So they also know that a drawing of a woolly rhinoceros must have been made before that time.

Other paintings show animals that no longer live in the area. For instance, reindeer used to live in certain regions, until a climate change caused them to move north. Thus, when scientists find a painting of a reindeer in a place where reindeer no longer live, they know that the painting was made before the climate changed.

The style of a drawing can also date it. Scientists know that Stone Age painters used certain styles and techniques during specific time periods. Scientists also date paintings by testing charcoal, bones, and other materials that artists left inside caves.

STONE AGE PAINT

To give cave paintings color, Stone Age people used minerals and other natural substances. A rock made of iron oxide left a red mark when scratched on a cave wall. A rock made of manganese oxide left a black mark. Other rocks left blue-black, dark brown, or white marks. By grinding rocks into a fine powder and mixing them with water or animal fat, Stone Age people made paints.

Soot from fires made a deep black paint. Berries and other plant parts provided more colors. Some Stone Age paints were very durable indeed. That's why we can still see the remains of cave paintings done more than 30,000 years ago.

MAGICAL PAINTINGS

Many people think that all caves have big openings that are easy to see and enter. In fact, many caves have secret entrances that are small and hard to find. Stone Age people probably had to crawl great distances, in pitch darkness, to reach some cave chambers. This must have been both scary and dangerous. In addition, some caves were home to dangerous bears, lions, bats, snakes, and bloodsucking insects. Since people went to so much trouble to enter and paint inside caves, we know that cave painting must have been very important for Stone Age people.

In fact, some scientists think that cave painting was not just a form of communication in ancient times but also a form of magic. Perhaps Stone Age people painted scenes of hunters killing mastodons as a way to wish for a successful hunt. Archaeologists have found hollow animal bones that were used to hold Stone Age paint. Perhaps people thought that paint stored in a mastodon bone contained the animal's spirit—and that it could bring luck to the hunters.

Other containers used to hold paint include hollow stones, large shells—even human skulls. Chemical tests show that these containers once held paint, although it long ago was used up or dried out.

EARLY PAINTING TECHNIQUES

What was the first paintbrush? A person's finger. The earliest cave paintings contain thick lines, made by an index finger dipped into paint, then rubbed on the cave wall. Artists also used their fingers to make outlines of animals, then they filled in the outlines.

But some lines in cave paintings are very fine and could not have been made with a finger. Archaeologists think that these marks were made with sharpened sticks or bird feathers that were dipped into paint like quill pens.

The first paintbrush with bristles was probably made from a twig. The artist probably chewed the end of the twig to separate the fibers. When dry, the fibers made a brush that could be used to transfer paint from the jar to the cave wall.

Stone Age people didn't have spray cans, but they still made spray paintings. On some cave walls, archaeologists have found outlines of human hands that must have been made with sprayed paint. How was it done? The artist probably placed a hand on a rock surface, took a mouthful of paint, and sprayed it out between the lips. In some cave paintings, sprayed paints show a blend of colors. Don't even think of imitating cave spray painters—modern paints are poisonous!

Sometimes cave painters drew the outlines of figures and left the insides empty. Other times, they filled in the outlines with a stamp dipped in paint and then daubed onto the rock. Stamps were probably made from animal fur, dried moss, or sticks chewed at one end to fray the fibers.

Stone Age artists sometimes made whole paintings from a series of small colored dots placed close together. Modern printers use the same kind of technology to reproduce photographs in newspapers. If you look very closely at a photograph in the daily newspaper, you'll see that the image is made from hundreds of closely spaced dots.

STONE AGE CRAYONS AND CHALK

Cave artists also made images with dry materials, including charcoal, which comes from burned wood. Charcoal is still a favorite with modern artists.

Some ancient artists drew with calcium carbonate, a form of limestone, also called chalk. Chunks of chalk, scraped against a stone surface, left grayish white marks, much like the chalk used on school blackboards. Modern chalk is made from calcium carbonate and several other ingredients.

ENGRAVINGS

Many Stone Age drawings were made by engraving—cutting lines into a surface such as a cave wall or a piece of stone, bone, antler, or ivory. To make the lines, Stone Age artists used a tool called a burin. It was a piece of very hard rock, perhaps flint, with a sharp tip. Burins of different sizes and shapes were used to make different kinds of lines. Archaeologists have found worn and broken flint burins on the ground right below Stone Age engravings.

Stone Age artists also made images by pecking or chipping away bits of rock to form outlines. They probably used a pointed stone as a punch and hammered it carefully with a stone hammer. Artists may have drawn the outline first with chalk, then followed the pattern for chipping away bits of rock.

Engraving of human figures from the Addaura cave, Italy

Pecked engravings took a long time to make. Most have been found on flat, horizontal surfaces, where an artist could have sat comfortably while working.

One Thing Leads to Another

New technology often emerges when people combine several kinds of existing technology. Stone Age artists developed a beautiful new form of communication, colored engraving, by combining painting and engraving. Artists usually began by engraving an outline or image on a rock surface. Then they applied a thin coat of paint that made the engraved lines more visible. Some of the most famous cave paintings were made in this way. One is a picture of a witch doctor—part human, part animal—found in the Trois-Frères cave in France.

ANCIENT MIDDLE EAST

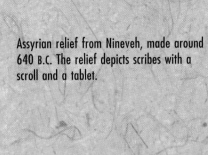

Assyrian relief from Nineveh, made around
640 B.C. The relief depicts scribes with a
scroll and a tablet.

Around **3500 B.C.,** people in the ancient Middle East began to abandon the hunter-gatherer lifestyle. They settled in a region known as the Fertile Crescent, an arc of fertile land extending from the eastern Mediterranean Sea to the Persian Gulf. There, people grew grain, vegetables, and fruit. They tamed wild animals and built homes, farms, and cities.

Among the many groups who lived in the ancient Middle East were the Sumerians, Babylonians, Hittites, Phoenicians, and Assyrians. These groups were very successful at growing food. For the first time in history, humans had extra food—a surplus—that they could sell to others.

ONE TECHNOLOGY LEADS TO ANOTHER

As Middle Eastern cities grew, and as people produced more food and other products, they could no longer rely on just brainpower to help them remember things. Government officials had to keep track of laws and who had paid taxes. Farmers needed a record of how much land they owned and how much grain and other food they had produced. Merchants and other businesspeople needed records of the goods they sold and debts owed to them. This new need for record keeping led to a new kind of communication technology—writing.

Archaeologists have found remains of written records, dating from 3300 B.C., in the city of Erech, in a region of the ancient Middle East known as Mesopotamia. The writings, made on clay tablets, included lists of grain that had been bought and sold, lists of jobs given to workers, delivery dates for goods, documents showing landownership, and other business records.

Some experts think that writing was invented by one person. We don't know the person's name, but it could have been a man, woman, or child who set out to keep records that were too long or too complicated to memorize. Other scholars think that a group of people in Erech invented writing. They might have been government officials or businesspeople who needed a good way to keep records. Another theory is that writing developed gradually over a span of many hundreds of years.

WRITING ON CLAY

The environment in which people live often determines the kind of technology they use. For instance, ancient Mesopotamia had few plants suitable for making paper. But the area had lots of high-quality clay. People used the clay to make building materials such as bricks and to store information.

Modern people store information on paper, computer

disks, and CDs. Mesopotamians stored their data on clay tablets—pieces of smooth clay small enough to fit into the palm of an adult's hand. When a clay tablet was damp, people could scratch pictures and letters into its surface using a sharpened reed. When dried in the hot sun, the clay hardened, preserving the writing and the information.

Sometimes the clay tablets were fired—heated like pottery—so they became very hard and waterproof. Firing created a longer-lasting document. Archaeologists have found many clay tablets from ancient Mesopotamia that are still in perfect condition.

CUNEIFORM

Writing on wet clay with a sharpened reed must have been messy and difficult. Try using a pencil point to make a fine line on wet clay. The point will create a big groove with raised edges that smear easily.

This technique must have frustrated the first writers in ancient Mesopotamia. So they found a solution—a better way of recording data on wet clay. The system was called cuneiform, which means "wedge shaped."

Using cuneiform, writers in Mesopotamia pressed lines straight down into clay with a special reed pen. The pen made indentations in the clay with no raised edges. Cuneiform was such a good technology that civilizations throughout the ancient Middle East adopted it. It was used to write more than 15 languages for more than 1,500 years.

WRITING IN PICTURES

The first kind of writing was picture-writing. Pictures used for writing are called pictograms. Pictograms showed images

Clay tablet inscribed with cuneiform writing, with its envelope, from El Quitar, Syria

from everyday life: grain, tools, fish, birds, and other animals and objects. Pictograms also expressed action, like the verbs in modern writing. For instance, a picture of a person's mouth combined with a picture of food meant "to eat." A picture of an eye accompanied by lines or dots stood for crying. A picture of a foot and mountains stood for traveling to the mountains.

Pictograms worked fairly well as symbols for familiar objects, but they weren't very good for describing new objects or complicated actions. Gradually pictograms changed shape. They became abstract—meaning they no longer looked like the objects they represented. Instead, writers had to memorize the meaning of each symbol—eventually more than two thousand in all.

Gradually people in the ancient Middle East began to use pictures to stand for *sounds* instead of for objects or ideas. This system was the first alphabet—a set of written symbols, each representing a sound, that could be combined to form words. With an alphabet, people could write any word in a language and invent new words to stand for new objects and ideas.

THE MOTHER ALPHABET

Who developed the first alphabet? Nobody knows. Many scholars have studied the alphabet for years without finding proof of its origins. Maybe the inventor was a very smart child who was just starting to learn cuneiform. He or she might then have realized that there was a simpler way of expressing words.

The first known alphabet is called the North Semitic alphabet, named after the Semites, people who once lived in modern-day Israel and Lebanon. Many experts think the alphabet originated between 1700 and 1500 B.C.

The North Semitic alphabet was the basis for other alphabets. By about 1000 B.C., four variations—the South Semitic, Canaanite, Aramaic, and Greek alphabets—were in use. The Phoenicians adopted a form of the Canaanite alphabet. It used 24 symbols that could be combined to express words. This alphabet, passed on to the Greeks and Romans, eventually became our English alphabet.

ANCIENT BEST-SELLERS

Ancient people used the new technology of writing not only for business and legal records but also to entertain and teach. One of the most famous ancient books is the Bible, which describes life in ancient Israel and contains the teachings of both the Jewish and Christian religions.

One of the oldest "thrillers," the *Epic of Gilgamesh*, was written in southern Mesopotamia before 2000 B.C. According to this story, Gilgamesh was a wicked king in Sumeria who was cruel to his subjects. The gods sent a hero, Enkidu, to kill Gilgamesh. Instead, the two men became friends and shared many adventures. When Enkidu died, Gilgamesh became afraid of death and searched for a way to live forever. The story ends with a great flood that destroys everything in the world.

At first the tale was passed along orally, by storytellers who memorized it. Later it was written on clay tablets. The earliest written version was discovered in 1853 at the ruins of an ancient palace in modern-day Iraq. The story was written on 12 tablets found in the palace library. Archaeologists have also found clay tablets containing the tale in other parts of the Middle East.

DEAD SEA SCROLLS

One day in 1947, a young shepherd was tending a flock of sheep in the rugged desert near Khirbat Qumran, in the

Section from *The Manual of Discipline,* one of the Dead Sea Scrolls

modern country of Jordan on the northwest shore of the Dead Sea. The shepherd found the opening to a cave and thought it might be interesting to explore inside. It was! There he found ancient manuscripts that had been hidden away for almost two thousand years. Scholars named them the Dead Sea Scrolls.

During the next 20 years, about six hundred similar manuscripts were found in other caves. The manuscripts had been written on papyrus (a material similar to paper), leather, and sheets of copper between 200 B.C. and A.D. 68.

Part of the library of the local Jewish people, the manuscripts consisted of rule books for the community, writings
about the Bible and religion, copies of almost every book in
the Old Testament, and other documents.

The scrolls were one of the most important finds in
modern archaeology. They gave scholars a wealth of new
information about the origins of the Bible and life in the
ancient Middle East. Archaeologists believe that the Jews
hid the scrolls in caves for safekeeping when the Roman
army invaded the region between 73 and 67 B.C.

3

ANCIENT EGYPT

Civilization in Egypt developed along the Nile River, which flows from the mountains of modern Uganda and Tanzania to the Mediterranean Sea. Ancient hunters and gatherers, seeking an abundant water supply, moved toward the Nile around 8000 B.C.

By around 7000 B.C., people had built permanent settlements along the river. In addition to providing water for crops and drinking, the Nile overflowed its banks every year, depositing a thick layer of muck that fertilized the soil.

Many plants grew along the shores of the Nile. One plant that grew in abundance along the Nile would change the history of human communication. It was the papyrus plant, sometimes called the paper plant.

PAPER = PAPYRUS

Papyrus, the root of our word *paper*, grows in creeks and rivers, sometimes as high as 15 feet. It has a triangular stem that may be more than two inches wide. It was these stems that the ancient Egyptians turned into paper.

Papermakers cut the stems into narrow strips and scraped away the inner layers of fiber. They placed several strips side by side, with the edges barely touching, to form a long narrow rectangle. Shorter strips were spread on top, at right angles to the strips beneath. The papermakers then wet the strips with water, beat them with hammers, and pressed them under heavy weights. The pressure caused sticky sap to flow from the plant fibers, sealing the two layers like glue. The sheets were left to dry, then polished. The resulting pieces of papyrus were bright white and smooth. Papermakers usually glued several sheets together to form long rolls. Many of the rolls were about 33 feet long, but some were as long as 100 feet. When the rolls were made right, the seams between the pages were almost invisible.

From Egypt, papyrus spread to other ancient countries, including Greece and Rome. But the material was expensive and precious. In many countries, the king decided who could make it. The Egyptian word *pa-en-per-aa*, the root of the word *papyrus*, means "that which belongs to the king."

In the fourth century A.D., people developed better writing surfaces—parchment and vellum, both made from animal skins. In the eighth century, the Western world learned the Chinese method of making paper from plant fibers. But papyrus was still used in some books until the 1200s.

The Pen

The first pens that scientists can date exactly were sharpened reeds, used by Egyptian scribes, or scholars, around 300 B.C. Using such pens was slow and tiresome, however.

The tools of an Egyptian scribe

The scribe dipped the tip of the pen into ink and moved it to the paper. Usually, the tip held enough ink for only a few strokes. Then it needed another dip, and another, and another. The point of the pen wore down quickly. It had to be sharpened frequently.

HIEROGLYPHICS

The Egyptian system of picture-writing, or hieroglyphics, is probably the most famous kind of ancient writing. The word *hieroglyphic* comes from two Greek terms: *hieros*, meaning "sacred," and *glyphein*, meaning "to carve."

Three commonly used
modern pictograms

Modern Hieroglyphics

Surprisingly, hieroglyphic writing has not completely died out. Modern people are returning to picture-writing more and more. Pictograms, or picture signs, are everywhere. They point the way to public rest rooms, telephones, emergency exits, and baggage-claim areas in airports. A picture of a cigarette with a slash through it means smoking is prohibited. A road sign with a curvy line means that the road turns ahead.

Pictograms are popular because more and more people are traveling to foreign countries. Even people who don't know a foreign language must still be able to read important signs. Pictograms give people information without written words.

In the 1970s, the U.S. Department of Transportation made a list of 34 pictograms for airports and other places used by travelers. Some language experts call these signs "modern hieroglyphics." They believe pictograms could lead to a new writing system that everyone in the world could understand. The system would use symbols that are not related to any one language. Other experts believe that such a system could never express the wide range of ideas put forth by a regular written language. What do you think?

For centuries, beginning around 3100 B.C., only priests used hieroglyphic writing. It was called "the speech of the gods" and was used for religious writings only. Later, merchants and other writers used the system. The symbols were sometimes written on papyrus and sometimes carved in stone with metal chisels.

Egyptian hieroglyphic writing used two kinds of symbols—ideograms and phonograms. Ideograms were pictures representing a specific object or idea. A drawing of the sun, for instance, meant "sun" or "day." Phonograms were "sound signs"—pictures that stood for sounds. By combining ideograms and phonograms, Egyptian writers could express many different ideas.

Hieroglyphic writing used hundreds of different symbols and was very difficult to learn. In English, we always write from left to right across a page and from top to bottom. Hieroglyphic symbols could be written from left to right or right to left, and from top to bottom or bottom to top.

Other Ways of Writing

After developing hieroglyphics, the ancient Egyptians created two other kinds of writing. These were cursive systems called hieratic and demotic. Cursive is longhand or script—the kind of writing children learn after they master printing.

Unlike hieroglyphics, hieratic and demotic writing consisted of symbols rather than pictures. Both forms were written on papyrus with a reed pen and ink. Both were written from left to right and top to bottom. Scribes could write in hieratic faster than in hieroglyphics because the system had fewer symbols, and they were simpler. Demotic was even simpler and faster. Scribes used hieratic to write letters, stories, business documents, and other records. Demotic was often used for legal documents.

THE ROSETTA STONE

By the sixth century A.D., people no longer practiced the ancient Egyptian religion. The last of the ancient temples had closed, and the priests had died. Egyptians themselves forgot how to read hieroglyphics. Most people thought the pictures were just religious symbols, not real writing.

The French emperor Napoleon invaded Egypt in 1798. In 1799 French soldiers at the village of Rashid, or Rosetta, discovered a big stone plaque inscribed with three kinds of writing. The soldiers knew that the stone was an important find, and they shipped it to Cairo. From there, the French made copies of the stone and sent them to scholars throughout Europe. The Rosetta stone weighed about 1,500 pounds, and to scholars it was worth its weight in gold. It was carved with hieroglyphics on top, demotic writing in the middle, and Greek on the bottom.

Scholars quickly translated the Greek and found the words to be a decree, issued in 196 B.C. by Ptolemy V, king of Egypt. The decree was written in Greek because the Greeks ruled Egypt at the time of the writing. Scholars realized that the other kinds of writing carried the same decree. They began comparing Greek words with the hieroglyphics at the top of the stone. They found hieroglyphic symbols for Greek names like Ptolemy and gradually learned how to translate hieroglyphics into Greek.

Deciphering the Rosetta stone took years of effort. A French expert, Jean-François Champollion, completed the work in 1823. What good was the Rosetta stone? It allowed archaeologists to translate hieroglyphic inscriptions on ancient Egyptian tombs and to learn all about ancient Egyptian civilization. Finding and translating the Rosetta stone was one of the greatest advances in archaeology.

HOT CAREER: SCRIBE

Education was important in ancient times, just as it is in modern times. The ability to communicate in writing made a big difference in a young person's life. People who knew how to read, write, and do arithmetic could become scribes, one of the best jobs in the ancient world.

Scribes wrote down orders and records for government officials and merchants, copied documents, and helped explain laws and religious rules. In Egypt, scribes had to master hieroglyphic, hieratic, and demotic writing. After

The Rosetta stone

Greece conquered Egypt, scribes also had to learn Greek so they could work for their new rulers. Scribes usually went to school, then served as apprentices, working with experienced scribes for a period of years to perfect their skills.

The life of a scribe was very nice. Scribes worked in clean, safe conditions, usually in palaces. They earned lots of money, did not have to pay taxes, and were excused from hard, dangerous projects like building pyramids. One ancient Egyptian papyrus describes a father urging his child to become a scribe. "The profession of scribe is a princely profession," the man said. "His writing materials and his rolls of books bring pleasantness and riches." Almost every ancient civilization had scribes, starting with Mesopotamia.

LIMESTONE SCRAP PAPER

Between 1550 and 1100 B.C., Egyptian rulers were buried in a special cemetery called the Valley of the Kings. Scribes, artists, painters, draftsmen, and other skilled craftspeople who decorated tombs in the Valley of the Kings lived in a town called Deir el-Medina, near the city of Luxor.

While fewer than one in one hundred adults in ancient Egypt could read or write, almost all adult men in Deir el-Medina were literate. For scrap paper, they used flakes of limestone called ostraca. Their pens were sharp tools used to scratch on the stone.

Deir el-Medina was buried under desert sands three thousand years ago. But archaeologists digging at the site have found thousands of ostraca containing notes, "to do" lists, receipts for deliveries, and even love songs.

chapter four

ANCIENT INDIA AND CHINA

Two-thousand-year-old relief of Prince Siddhartha, who later founded the Buddhist religion, on his way to school. He is shown riding a ram, and his attendants are carrying his stool and writing implements.

In modern Pakistan, in the valleys around the Indus River, people began settling into farming villages around 4000 B.C. The settlements eventually became cities, and within a thousand years, one of the world's greatest civilizations began to emerge. We call it the Indus Valley civilization.

Like the ancient Middle East, the Indus Valley had fertile land that produced more than enough crops to feed the population. The surplus thus could be traded for metals, timber, dye, and other products. Trade required written records, road signs, and other forms of communication. The ancient Indians probably learned some communication technology from the Mesopotamians, with whom they traded.

GREAT BOOKS OF ANCIENT INDIA

The Vedic Age, a thousand-year period in ancient Indian history (1500–500 B.C.), was named for four great books, the Vedas. *Veda* means "knowledge" in Sanskrit, the language of ancient India. The Vedas are also called the Samhitas, meaning "the collections." They were written in Vedic, the earliest form of Sanskrit, at the end of the third century B.C.

The earliest and most important of the books, the *Rig Veda*, contains more than one thousand prayers, religious songs, and poems. The other books, the *Yajur Veda*, *Sama Veda*, and *Atharva Veda*, include magic spells, instructions for priests, and other materials. Some authors wrote books about the Vedas. Called commentaries, they describe the Vedas in greater detail.

Vedic Sanskrit developed around 1500 B.C. The word *sanskrit* means "adored" or "cultivated." Sanskrit began as a sacred language for priests, who were among the most highly educated people in ancient India. Another form of the language, classical Sanskrit, came into use around 500 B.C. Classical Sanskrit is still used by highly educated people in modern India.

BAD GRAMMAR? NO, FIRST GRAMMAR

Have you ever heard someone use bad grammar? Maybe the person said, "I ain't the one that done that." A grammar is a system of rules for using a language. It explains how nouns, pronouns, verbs, adverbs, and other parts of speech should be put together into proper sentences. The rules help us use language clearly and gracefully, without unnecessary or confusing words.

The earliest known grammar was developed for the Sanskrit language by an Indian scholar named Pānini, who lived around 400 B.C. Pānini not only listed rules for using Sanskrit, but he was also the first person to study grammar, to better understand how language works.

Emperor Asoka ordered an inscription on Buddhism to be engraved on this stone pillar in Sarnath, India.

HOW DO YOU GET TO...?

Signs, such as road signs, are an important form of communication. They are a type of mass communication—a way of sending messages to many people at the same time. Almost all ancient civilizations that had roads marked them with road signs.

Emperor Asoka, who ruled India from about 269 to 232 B.C., developed one of the first and best road-sign systems. He ordered that stone pillars be erected along the Royal Road, which stretched through India for 2,600 miles. The huge pillars were inscribed with directions for travelers. They also gave advice from Asoka, telling travelers to obey laws and to be good citizens.

ANCIENT CHINA

The ancient Chinese made some of the most important contributions to our communication technology, including the invention of paper, printing, and ink. Ancient China was also home to one of the world's most famous writers, Confucius, who lived from 551 to 479 B.C.

The Chinese developed a lot of communication technology in isolation. China was a remote country that had very little contact with other ancient civilizations, especially faraway places like Rome and Greece. The Chinese didn't know about papyrus, which was used as paper in ancient Egypt. China might have learned some communication technology from the Mesopotamians, however, with whom they sometimes traded.

WOOD, BAMBOO, AND SILK

The Chinese wrote on many different materials before learning to make paper. They wrote on flat pieces of wood and on strips of bamboo. They drilled holes in these "pages" and tied them together with string to make books—sort of like modern loose-leaf binders. These books didn't last very long, however, because wood and bamboo tend to crack and rot.

The Chinese also wrote on pieces of silk, made from the cocoons of silkworms. Silk was very expensive (and still is), and only the richest people could afford to use it for writing.

REAL PAPER

About 1,900 years ago, the Chinese developed one of our most basic communication tools—paper. Ts'ai Lun, minister of public works for the emperor Ho-Ti, made the first sheet of paper from the inner bark of the mulberry tree. Other sheets were made from bamboo, rice straw, even old rags and fishing nets.

Usually Chinese papermakers soaked bark or bamboo in water until it became very soft and was almost ready to fall apart. Then the fibers were separated by beating and stirring in water. This process resulted in a thick, soupy mixture called pulp. The pulp was spread on a screen the size of the desired piece of paper. As the pulp dried, the fibers stuck together, forming a sheet of paper.

For more than five hundred years, China was the only civilization to make paper this way. The rest of the world finally learned about paper in A.D. 751, when a Chinese army attacked Samarkand in Russia, which was then controlled by Middle Eastern people called Moors. The Moors defeated the Chinese and took many prisoners. Among them were papermakers, who showed the Moors their technology. Paper mills were set up in Baghdad in modern-day Iraq. Papermaking technology spread to Europe after the Moors conquered Spain and after the Crusaders, Christian armies from Europe, attacked Moorish lands.

PRINTING

One form of technology often leads to another. The Chinese invented paper; printing was the next logical step. Printing is a technique for producing multiple, indentical copies of a document.

In about A.D. 100, Chinese cloth makers began printing pictures and designs on fabric. They used a technique called block printing. They made designs on wooden blocks, carving away the background so that the pictures stood out. They put ink (also invented by the Chinese) on the raised images and pressed the blocks onto sheets of fabric.

Then Chinese printmakers used the same system with written words. They carved words into wooden blocks and transferred the ink and writing onto paper. Why had no one tried the technique on earlier types of paper? Papyrus was too fragile. Parchment and vellum, made from animal skins, were too expensive. But the paper developed by Ts'ai Lun was just right—both durable and affordable.

Chinese gold chops, or seals, made during the West Han dynasty (206 B.C. to A.D. 8)

Spreading the Word

Printing was a great advance in communication technology. It allowed people to copy books and other documents faster than ever before. Before the invention of printing, scribes sometimes had to write for months, just to copy a single book by hand. Since the process was so time consuming, few books were available. When a product is scarce, it also is expensive. During much of ancient times, books were so costly that only kings, emperors, and other wealthy people could afford them. Printing made books less costly and more available to common people.

Producing books by block printing was still expensive, however, because each page required a carved block. Once carved, the block could not be used to print anything else. In the eleventh century A.D., the Chinese improved printing even more with the invention of movable type—small metal blocks, each stamped with one letter of the alphabet or another symbol. Since each letter was separate, the blocks could be arranged to form any word and could be used again and again. Johannes Gutenberg, a German printer who lived from about 1390 to 1468, improved movable type and invented the modern printing press.

India Ink? Chinese Ink!

The Chinese made their first inks from animal blood, berries, tree bark, and other natural substances. Many plants contain tannins, chemicals that impart a pale yellow or light brown color to paper and other material. The Chinese used tannin from tea and other plants to make ink.

India ink is one of the finest inks used for writing. It is a velvety smooth ink that flows onto paper in rich black lines. Despite its name, India ink was actually developed in ancient China around 2500 B.C.

India ink was made from carbon black, a sooty material produced by burning tar, pitch, or even bones. Chinese ink makers mixed carbon black with glues and gums and poured the mixture into molds in the shape of sticks. After the mixture dried, a writer would break off a piece of ink stick and dip it in water to use as a pen.

Nobody is sure how India ink got the wrong name. People in ancient Greece, Rome, and the Middle East didn't know much about remote lands like India and China and may have considered them all the same.

ANCIENT BOOK BURNER

Have you ever heard the term *book burner?* Throughout history, some closed-minded people have burned books because they didn't like the writers' messages or opinions. One of the earliest known book burners was Shih Huang Ti, the first emperor of China. In 213 B.C., he ordered that all books in China be burned, except those dealing with medicine, farming, or predicting the future. Why? Shih Huang Ti wanted to make China a more modern country, and he believed that books with old ideas would hold back progress. Many people refused to comply with the order, and lots of old books survived.

When Shih Huang Ti took power in China in 221 B.C., people in different parts of the huge country used different pictograms to stand for the same words. As a result, people in one area couldn't understand the writing of people in another. Shih Huang Ti wanted to unify all of China into one country and to make sure that everyone understood his

Eighteenth-century
engraving of Emperor
Shih Huang Ti, based
on an undated
painting

orders. So he ordered everyone to use the same set of
about three thousand pictograms. This same writing system
is still in use in China, more than two thousand years later.

CONFUCIUS SAID

One of the most famous Chinese writers was Confucius, a
philosopher who lived from 551 to 479 B.C. In Chinese his
name was K'ung-Fu-tzu. Confucius spent most of his adult
life as a police official in his home province. He was known

for encouraging people to live honest lives and to treat others in an ethical way.

At age 57, Confucius began writing down his ideas and sayings. His followers gathered them into a book called *The Analects*. Most of Confucius's sayings were very serious and practical. One was: "To store up knowledge in silence, to remain forever hungry for learning, to teach others without tiring—all this comes to me naturally." Another: "I transmit, I invent nothing. I trust and love the past."

5

ANCIENT AMERICAS

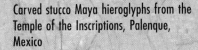

Carved stucco Maya hieroglyphs from the Temple of the Inscriptions, Palenque, Mexico

The Americas, also called the New World, were home to many ancient civilizations. American Indians, a name given to hundreds of native tribes by European settlers, lived throughout North America as early as 10,000 years ago. Mexico and Central America (called Mesoamerica) were home to a number of ancient civilizations, including the Olmec and the Maya.

With few written records remaining, we know very little about how people in the ancient Americas communicated. But we do know that the Maya, the most advanced Mesoamerican civilization, developed a complete system of writing.

AMERICAN WRITERS

Several civilizations in ancient America, including the Olmec and the Zapotec, used symbols to record events and thoughts. But the Maya were the only people to develop an actual writing system. They wrote books, painted inscriptions on pottery and walls, and carved words into stone monuments. Many inscriptions were carved on stelae, rectangular slabs of stone set upright like signs.

Maya writing was much like Egyptian hieroglyphic writing. It consisted of more than eight hundred glyphs, or symbols, showing faces, animals, and other objects. Each glyph carried a meaning, and glyphs could be combined to form words or ideas. Glyphs were drawn inside squares and arranged in columns, read from top to bottom. Archaeologists have deciphered many Maya glyphs, but understanding them is very difficult. The same glyph can represent several different sounds and ideas.

Was it just a coincidence that the ancient Maya developed hieroglyphic writing like the ancient Egyptians did? Or could the ancient Egyptians have somehow met the Maya and taught them how to use hieroglyphics? Those questions may sound silly. But some historians have argued that the Maya could not have developed writing on their own. After all, the Maya were a Stone Age people who did not use advanced technology such as wheels or metal tools. The scholars wondered whether sailors from Egypt or another country could have traveled to Central America and taught the Maya writing.

Most archaeologists reject this idea. They believe that civilizations in different parts of the world can develop technology independently, without outside help. Often two different civilizations stumble on similar technological solutions. The Egyptians and the Maya both needed a way to record events. Both realized that picture-writing suited their needs.

Accordion Books

The ancient Maya wrote on long sheets of a paperlike material made from the inner bark of fig trees that grew in the rain forest. Some sheets were more than 20 feet long. They were covered with a white paint made from powdered limestone, water, and other materials.

Priests and scribes wrote glyphs on the sheets with black ink made from a sootlike material. They also drew colored pictures to illustrate the glyphs. Each sheet was then folded into pleats, much like the folds in an accordion, to make a kind of book called a codex.

The destruction of the land of Mu, described in the *Codex Troano*

Smoke Signals and Sign Language

Did ancient Native Americans communicate with sign language and smoke signals like they do in cowboy-and-Indian movies? We don't know the answer. But both systems are very effective ways of communicating.

Sign language is a communication system based on hand and other gestures. It is a visual system that passes on information without speech. During the 1800s, Native Americans on the Great Plains used a language called Plains Indian Sign Talk to communicate with groups who spoke different languages. Smoke signals and fires were used in ancient times in Europe for long-distance communication. But without written or other evidence, we can't be sure whether these methods were used in ancient times in North America.

LIBRARIES

Archaeologists think that the Maya kept big libraries that were probably housed in temples, since priests and rulers were the only people who could read. The libraries probably held books about religious topics and practical matters like farming, medicine, construction, and other forms of technology.

Many of the books rotted in the hot, wet rain forest climate. Others survived for centuries, however. In 1519, when Spanish explorers landed in Mexico, they found ancient books left by the Maya. Unfortunately, Spanish missionaries, attemping to convert native people to Christianity, thought the ancient books were evil and burned them. One missionary, Diego de Landa, wrote:

> These people also made use of certain characters or letters, with which they wrote in their books their ancient affairs and sciences. . . . We found a great number of books in these characters, and, as they contained nothing in which there was not to be superstition and lies of the devil, we burned them all, which they regretted to an amazing degree and which caused them affliction.

With the books burned, modern archaeologists have few clues to help them understand ancient Maya civilization and to decipher the Maya glyphs. Of thousands of ancient Maya books, only three and bits of a fourth have survived.

PAINTED WALLS

Besides being writers, the Maya were artists who painted beautiful pictures on pottery and walls of temples. Murals discovered at one ancient Maya settlement, in Mexico near the border of Guatemala, provided valuable information about the Maya. Archaeologists named the settlement Bonampak, a Maya word meaning "painted walls."

Archaeologists discovered the settlement in the 1940s, overgrown with a tangle of jungle vegetation. One building had walls covered with colorful paintings showing warfare and warriors taking and killing prisoners.

The murals were a sensation. Until then, experts had thought that the Maya were a peace-loving people who seldom or never waged war. The murals helped archaeologists realize that warfare was an important part of Maya civilization and that previous ideas about the Maya were wrong.

TALKING STICKS AND TALKING CORDS

Have you ever written a "to do" list? Have you ever put notes for a classroom presentation on index cards? Ancient people in the Americas used "talking cords" and "talking sticks" to keep the same kinds of notes.

Talking cords were pieces of string or strips of leather tied into knots or loops that communicated a message. "Take this knotted rope when you fight the enemy," a king might have told his generals. "Untie one knot each day of the battle. If you haven't won when the last knot is untied, you may come back home." Ancient people in Peru used talking cords called quipus (pronounced "kee-pooz") for record keeping.

Talking sticks were similar. Notches cut into the sticks helped ancient people keep tallies and other records. Farmers and shepherds in some countries still use talking sticks and talking cords to keep track of their herds.

6

ANCIENT GREECE

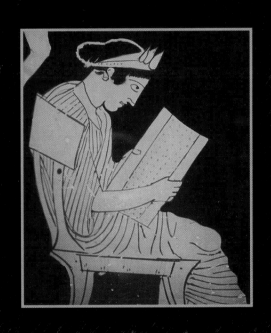

Ancient Greece was a great center of learning and communication. The Greeks wrote famous tragedies, comedies, histories, poems, and speeches that modern people still read and enjoy.

But few ancient people actually read these works. Instead, the poems and stories were spread orally—through speech. Actors and orators memorized the famous works and recited them to audiences. In this way, history, legend, and wisdom were passed from one generation to the next. Some information was not written down for hundreds of years.

Throughout the ancient world, very few people could read and write. In ancient Egypt, for instance, only about one in one hundred people were literate. Most ancient people had little need for written communication anyway. There were no newspapers or magazines. Common people rarely traveled, so they didn't need to read road signs. Written communication was important mainly for government officials, who kept track of laws, payrolls, and taxes, and for merchants, who kept business records.

But as ancient Greece became more involved with other countries, written communication became more important. Alexander the Great, who lived from 356 to 323 B.C., ruled Greece and many surrounding countries, including Egypt. It was difficult to keep track of the history and current events in these countries, where many different languages were spoken. Written records were the only way to deal with the flood of new information.

BORROWING FROM THE PHOENICIANS

After years of trading with the Phoenicians, Greek merchants became quite familiar with the Phoenician alphabet. Around 800 B.C., the Greeks began to use it to write their own language. They borrowed 19 of the Phoenicians' 22 letters. They also added a few new letters, including phi and psi, to represent sounds missing from the Phoenician alphabet.

Although the Greeks kept the Phoenician symbols, they changed the pronunciations. The Phoenician symbol "aleph" was renamed "alpha," and it became the first letter of the Greek alphabet. The symbol "beth" was changed to "beta," and it became the second letter. By combining these two names, the Greeks coined the word *alphabet*.

At first the Greeks wrote like the Phoenicians, from right to left, though they sometimes changed direction. This method was called *boustrophedon*, meaning "like an ox turning." It referred to the way farmers plowed a field with oxen, moving one way down a row, then turning and plowing the next row in the opposite direction. The Greeks also flipped letters around sometimes so they faced in the opposite direction. Around 500 B.C., the Greeks adopted a standard writing direction, from left to right. Around 400 B.C., they adopted a standard 24-letter alphabet in which letters always faced in the same direction.

BOOKS WITHOUT PAGES

Mention ancient papyruses and most people think of the long scrolls that the ancient Egyptians used as books. But the ancient Greeks and Romans wrote on papyrus, too. Greek writers mention papyrus as early as the sixth century B.C., and more than 30,000 Greek papyrus scrolls have survived to modern times. Some date to the fourth century B.C.

The Greeks were very practical bookmakers—they wanted to fit as much information as possible on each scroll. Whereas the Egyptians often wrote in fancy lettering that took up lots of room, the Greeks wrote in small letters. They wrote in columns about three inches wide, with space between columns and margins on each side of the page. The Egyptians sometimes added drawings as decorations on their scrolls. But the Greeks used only drawings that communicated information—such as a diagram that showed how a machine worked.

The Greeks wanted to keep scrolls small enough for readers to hold them comfortably. The typical Greek scroll was about 33 feet long. Rolled up, it was about 2 inches in diameter and 9 or 10 inches high. Readers didn't turn pages, they just unrolled the scroll—usually unrolling with the right hand while rewinding with the left hand. Some scrolls had a wooden roller with knobs to help keep scrolls neatly wound.

Each scroll was called a *volumen,* a Latin word from which we get the English word *volume.* The scrolls were very expensive because there were no printing presses in ancient Greece. Each scroll was written by hand.

WHAT A LIBRARY!

The most famous library in the ancient world was located in the city of Alexandria in Egypt. The Greeks built the library (and founded the city) after they conquered Egypt in 322 B.C. A Greek leader named Ptolemy Soter, king of Egypt, planned the library. It was built by his son, Ptolemy II.

The most famous writers and scholars of the day ran the library. They wanted to collect the best Greek literature, as well as knowledge from the rest of the world, in one place. Over the years, the library collected more and more books—probably between one hundred thousand and seven hundred thousand—including the biggest collection of medical books in the world.

"STUFF FROM PERGAMOS"

Books were so important in ancient Greece that two rulers, Ptolemy V and Eumenes II of Pergamos, almost went to war over them. Ptolemy wanted the library at Alexandria to be the world's biggest. Eumenes wanted his own library, located at Pergamos in the modern country of Turkey, to have the most books. Each ruler tried to make more books than the other.

Worried that Eumenes was getting ahead, Ptolemy banned the shipment of papyrus from Egypt to Pergamos. So Eumenes needed a new technology for recording words on paper. He developed parchment, a heavy paperlike material made from the skins of animals. In Latin and Greek, *parchment* means "stuff from Pergamos."

Other ancient people had written on animal skins before Eumenes developed parchment. Scribes in ancient Mesopotamia may have done so. Records show that the Egyptians used leather as a writing surface in 2450 B.C. But leather, made by a different process than parchment, was not very good for writing. It was thick and dark and rotted easily. Parchment was different. It was light in color, flexible, and long lasting.

Parchment was made from the skins of sheep, goats, and cattle. Workers first removed all the hair and flesh. Then they stretched the skins tightly in wooden frames. The skins were treated on both sides with chalk to make them brighter. They were rubbed with pumice, a fine powder that made them silky smooth.

ONE THING LEADS TO ANOTHER

The development of parchment led, in the first century B.C., to the creation of modern books. Whereas papyrus was used to make books on scrolls, parchment was used for

Greek silver coin depicting King Ptolemy V

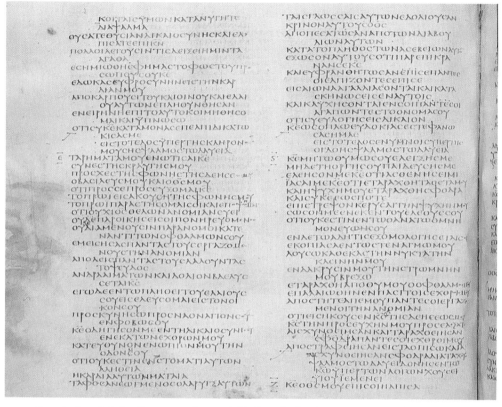

Reproduction of *Codex Sinaiticus,* a Christian Bible from the fourth century A.D. It is the earliest surviving Greek book.

books bound together in sheaves, like modern books. We call this kind of book a codex.

Parchment was ideal for making codices. With papyrus scrolls, the fibers of the papyrus plant were lined up in such a way that it was difficult to write on both sides. But with parchment, both sides could be used for writing. So one sheet of parchment could hold twice as much information as a sheet of papyrus of the same size. While papyrus was brittle, parchment was flexible. It could be folded into individual pages. One fold in a sheet made a "folio" of two pages. Two folds made a "quarto" of four pages. Three folds made an "octavo" of eight pages. Folded sheets were then cut and sewn together to form a book that opened page by page.

Codices were much easier to read than scrolls. A person could open a codex instantly to any page, without having to unroll foot after foot of papyrus. With writing on both sides of each sheet, a codex held much more text than a papyrus scroll, with more room for illustrations.

People often adopt new technology slowly—even if the new technology, such as parchment and codices, is far superior to the old. Even after the introduction of parchment, people still used papyrus scrolls. It was not until the fourth century A.D. that parchment became the ancient world's main writing material. Even so, papyrus scrolls were often used for official government documents until the A.D. 900s. Parchment later was replaced by paper.

THE TELEGRAPH: A BRIGHT OLD IDEA

In the 1790s, a French inventor named Claude Chappe became famous for setting up a telegraph system to send messages across France. Whereas some telegraph systems involve electric signals sent over wires, Chappe created a *visual* telegraph—he built stations within sight of each other. At the first station, a worker used a semaphore, or sign, to send a message to the next station. The person at the next station saw the sign and posted the same semaphore, sending the message on to yet another station. Eventually the message got all the way across France.

Chappe's idea was not new. Around 500 B.C., the Greeks began using a special system for sending messages from city to city. It was also a visual telegraph. The Greeks built a series of towers between big cities. Each tower was close enough to be seen easily from the next. Twenty-four holes at the tops of the towers represented letters in the Greek alphabet. By lighting fires in the right holes, Greeks could send simple messages, such as "Danger." This idea wasn't new either. For thousands of years, ancient people had been sending signals by building fires on hilltops.

RUNNERS: THE FIRST MARATHON

In the ancient world, runners were the fastest way of sending messages from one place to another. Military leaders, kings, government officials, and traders used runners just like we use Federal Express and other overnight delivery services. Runners sometimes carried written messages and sometimes memorized long spoken messages. They often had to swim rivers and climb hills and mountains. They had to be all-around athletes with good memories.

In 490 B.C., during the Persian Wars, a Persian army landed at Marathon, about 25 miles north of Athens, and was defeated by a smaller Greek force. The Greeks wanted to get news of the victory to Athens right away. According to legend, they turned to their fastest runner, who had just returned from a long run. Still he took the mission, ran to Athens, cried out, "Rejoice, we are victorious," and died of exhaustion. The modern marathon, 26 miles, 385 yards, was named in his honor.

ANCIENT ROME

Ancient Rome, a civilization based in Italy and eventually extending throughout much of Europe and the Mediterranean world, made many advances in communication technology. Perhaps most important, Rome gave us the Latin language, which was, for centuries, the official language of governments and scholars throughout Europe. Latin also became the basis for many modern languages, including French, Italian, and Spanish.

The first traces of Latin appear in inscriptions made in the sixth century B.C. Several different forms of Latin were used, including early or archaic Latin, classical Latin, and Golden Latin. Ordinary Roman people, who had little education, spoke an informal kind of Latin. We know about it mainly from graffiti—often nasty words that people wrote on walls. Educated people in Rome usually learned both Latin and Greek, since many books were written in Greek. As Rome's armies conquered other countries and established the Roman Empire, Latin spread throughout Europe.

THE MODERN ALPHABET

How do better forms of technology appear? Often one civilization borrows and improves upon the technology developed in an earlier civilization. That certainly is the story of our modern alphabet. It developed from the Latin alphabet used in ancient Rome.

The Latin alphabet was a lot like our English alphabet, except it had only 23 letters. The missing letters—J, U, and

Stela, or inscribed stone, from the first century A.D. The letters on the stela have serifs.

W—were added later. Latin was based on an alphabet used by the Etruscans, who ruled northern Italy from the eighth to the fifth centuries B.C. Where did the Etruscans get their alphabet? They modeled it after the Greek alphabet. As their model, the Greeks used an alphabet developed around 1000 B.C. by the Phoenicians. The Phoenician alphabet was based on the earliest known alphabet, North Semitic, developed around 1700 B.C. in the ancient Middle East.

BEAUTIFUL LETTERS

Take a close look at the letters you're reading in this book. Do you notice the little "feet" on the bottom, top, and sides of some of the letters? These "feet" are actually called serifs.

Serifs make it easier to read lines of type on a page by leading our eyes from one letter to the next. Serifs also add a touch of beauty and class to letters. Letters without serifs are called sans serif (*sans* means "without"). Who developed this technology for improving the way people read? The ancient Romans.

CURSIVE WRITING

In the fourth century B.C., Roman scribes developed an efficient way of writing called cursive, or longhand. Instead of writing separate letters of the alphabet with spaces between them, scribes joined the letters together with curved, flowing lines. They could write much faster in cursive, continuing right across a sheet of paper with fewer pauses. The first form of cursive, Old Roman Cursive, was used for about one hundred years. It was replaced by New Roman Cursive, which developed into modern cursive.

One big difference between ancient Roman writing and

our own is that the Romans rarely used commas or other punctuation. Spaces between words also were rare—one word usually ran right into the next word. Capital letters were used infrequently, except in some headings and addresses.

TIME SAVERS

Abbreviations and acronyms make written communication simpler. When addressing a letter, for instance, it is easier to write the abbreviation *MN* than the full word *Minnesota*. The acronym *CJHS* is easier to write than "Central Junior High School."

The ancient Romans developed hundreds of abbreviations and acronyms. VCCC, for example, was short for *viri clarissimi* ("a most-distinguished gentleman"). PR meant *populus Romanus* ("the Roman people"). OHSS meant *ossa hic sita sunt* ("The bones lie here").

WRITING MATERIALS

Papyrus was scarce in parts of the Roman Empire, including northern Italy, so people sometimes wrote on tree bark. In fact, the Latin word for book is *liber*, which means "bark." The Romans also wrote on very thin sheets of wood peeled from trees. Each sheet was called a leaf, a word we still use to mean a page in a book. Sometimes people cut holes in the sheets and fastened them together with string to form tablets, sort of like modern pads of paper. Bark and wood dried out and rotted very quickly, however. So they were used for writing letters and lists that didn't have to last long.

For important records that had to last, the ancient

Roman writing materials, including a stylus, seals, and a reproduction of a wax tablet

Romans sometimes wrote on wax tablets. The tablets were made from pieces of wood that looked like modern picture frames. They had raised edges, and the centers were filled with beeswax. Writers used a pointed wooden stick, called a stylus, to scratch letters and numbers in the wax.

Wax tablets had holes in the edges so that several could be bound together with rings, like those used in modern loose-leaf binders. When the tablets were closed, the raised edges protected the wax from damage. Wax tablets were often stored in special bronze boxes.

LIBRARIES

Libraries in the ancient world were usually found in palaces, temples, and the homes of very rich people. Some library owners let friends borrow books.

Books were considered treasures in ancient times, and soldiers sometimes brought them home from countries they had conquered. A Roman general, Lucius Licinius Lucullus, built a huge home library of books he had taken from conquered lands. It became a gathering place and a study for famous Roman and Greek writers like Cicero, Cato, and Plutarch.

The first public library was built around 40 B.C. in Rome by a rich man named Gaius Asinius Pollio. The library was located in the Hall of Liberty, and it contained thousands of Roman and Greek books. The Roman historian Pliny described the library with a phrase that some libraries still use as a motto: *Ingenia hominum rem publicam*—"He made men's talents a public possession."

Roman emperors eventually built many other public libraries. They were often gifts to cities and towns, a way to help keep citizens loyal to the emperor.

HUMAN PRINTING PRESSES

With no printing presses, books had to be copied by hand in ancient Rome. Roman book publishers saw that it was very inefficient for one person to copy one book, though. So publishers hired people called readers and copyists.

To create multiple copies of books, a reader would

slowly read a book to a room full of as many as 30 copyists. They would write each word, making many copies of a book at the same time. This method made books cheaper to produce. As books became less expensive, more middle-class people could buy them.

First Daily Newspaper

The world's first daily newspaper was probably *Acta Diurna* (*Daily Events*), published in ancient Rome. Emperor Julius Caesar started *Acta Diurna* in 59 B.C. as a way to keep citizens informed of government decrees, new laws, and important events. But the paper also included human-interest items, such as notices of births and deaths.

Unlike modern newspapers, *Acta Diurna* was handwritten. Remember, there were no printing presses in ancient Rome. Only a few copies of the paper were made. They were posted in public places so that many people could read them.

"Neither Snow, Nor Rain, Nor Heat . . ."

Many ancient civilizations developed postal systems for sending mail and other messages quickly over long distances. Rulers needed these systems to keep in touch with all parts of their empires. They used a relay system, in which couriers were stationed at different posts separated by a distance that a man or horse could run before tiring. At each relay station, the courier passed his message to a fresh runner or exchanged his tired horse for a new one. In this way, messages always traveled at top speed.

Couriers sometimes traveled more than one hundred miles a day using this system. Nothing stopped them.

Around 400 B.C., the Greek historian Herodotus wrote this description of Persian couriers: "Neither snow, nor rain, nor heat, nor gloom of night stays these couriers." His words became the unofficial motto of modern postal systems.

Around 27 B.C., the Roman emperor Augustus Caesar developed the most advanced postal system in the ancient world. His couriers rode horses along Rome's famous paved roads, resting or passing their messages along at relay stations called post houses. Ancient postal systems were used mainly for government business. Around A.D. 200, the Roman postal system began carrying private messages, too.

A UNIVERSAL LANGUAGE

Latin remained in use throughout the Western world for almost two thousand years. It became the "universal language" of Europe, which all students learned along with their native languages. Using Latin, scientists and scholars could communicate with educated people from other countries. Diplomats and government officials could carry out negotiations with foreign leaders.

In a period of history known as the Renaissance, which began in Italy in the fourteenth century, almost all books were written in Latin. Latin remained the universal language until the eighteenth century, when it was replaced by French. Today English has become the universal language for science, business, and diplomacy.

Very New World Hieroglyphics

In the early 1970s, scientists built *Pioneer 10*, a space probe that would study Jupiter and Saturn and continue on into deep space. The scientists realized that someday an extraterrestrial civilization might find *Pioneer 10*, so they attached a message to a plaque on the probe's antenna.

What form of communication did the scientists pick for the message? Picture-writing, like that used by the ancient Maya and Egyptians. The scientists knew that beings from another planet would not understand any language used on Earth. So the message consisted of pictures and symbols.

The *Pioneer 10* plaque shows what male and female humans look like. The man's hand is raised in a gesture of goodwill. The plaque also shows our size. A design right behind the human figures shows the *Pioneer 10* antenna. By measuring the antenna's height, alien beings would be able to figure out human body proportions.

Circles at the bottom of the plaque (below) show that *Pioneer 10* was launched by people living on the third planet from the Sun—Earth—and show Earth's size compared to the Sun. Crossed lines show the Sun's position in our galaxy, the Milky Way. Two circles at the upper left corner of the plaque (above) show scientific information about hydrogen, the most common chemical element in the universe.

Glossary

abbreviation—a shortened form of a written word or phrase

acronym—a word formed from the first letters of words in a compound term

alphabet—a set of letters and characters that make up a written language

codex—a book with individual pages

cuneiform—a writing system developed in the ancient Middle East, consisting of wedge-shaped characters

cursive—a style of writing in which letters are connected by flowing lines

demotic—a simplified form of Egyptian hieroglyphics

engraving—cutting lines or designs into a surface

glyph—a symbol or pictogram

grammar—a system of rules about how to use a language

hieratic—a simplified form of Egyptian hieroglyphics

hieroglyphics—ancient Egyptian or Maya picture-writing

ideogram—a picture or symbol that represents an object or idea

ostraca—flakes of stone used by the ancient Egyptians as "scratch paper"

papyrus—an Egyptian plant made into paper in ancient times; paper made from the papyrus plant

parchment—the skin of a sheep or goat made into a writing surface

phonogram—a symbol used to represent a sound

pictogram—a picture used to represent an object or idea

scribe—an ancient writer or scholar

serifs—short lines on the ends of letters that make reading easier

telegraph—a system for long-distance communication

vellum—the skin of a lamb or calf made into a writing surface

SELECTED BIBLIOGRAPHY

Adkins, Lesley, and Roy A. Adkins. *Handbook to Life in Ancient Rome.* New York: Facts on File, 1994.

Beshore, George. *Science in Ancient China.* New York: Franklin Watts, 1998.

Clark, Ronald W. *Works of Man.* New York: Viking, 1985.

Giblin, James Cross. *The Riddle of the Rosetta Stone: Key to Ancient Egypt.* New York: Harper Collins, 1990.

Hooker, J. T. *Reading the Past: Ancient Writing from Cuneiform to the Alphabet.* Berkeley, CA: University of California Press, 1990.

Ingpen, Robert, and Philip Wilkinson. *Encyclopedia of Ideas That Changed the World: The Greatest Discoveries and Inventions of Human History.* New York: Penguin Books, 1993.

James, Peter, and Nick Thorpe. *Ancient Inventions.* New York: Ballantine Books, 1994.

Lauber, Patricia. *Painters of the Caves.* Washington, DC: National Geographic Society, 1998.

Martell, Hazel Mary. *Worlds of the Past: The Ancient Chinese.* New York: New Discovery Books, 1993.

Robinson, Andrew. *The Story of Writing: Alphabets, Hieroglyphs and Pictograms.* New York: Thames and Hudson, 1995.

Saggs, H. W. F. *Civilization Before Greece and Rome.* New Haven, CT: Yale University Press, 1989.

Woods, Geraldine. *Science in Ancient Egypt.* New York: Franklin Watts, 1998.

INDEX

Mesopotamia, 26–27, 30, 42, 45, 69
Middle East: archaeological evidence of writing, 26–27, 30–32; on clay, 26–27; cuneiform, 27; Dead Sea Scrolls, 30–32; in pictures, 27–29; record keeping, 25–26
murals, 61–62

newspaper, first daily, 81

paper, 35–36; Chinese papermaking, 49
papyrus, 31, 35–36, 67, 70–71
parchment, 68–71
pens, 36–37
Phoenicia, 10, 25, 30, 66, 77
phonograms, 39
pictograms, 27–29, 38, 53, 83. *See* glyphs; hieroglyphics
picture-writing. *See* pictograms
postal system, Roman origins, 81–82
printing, 49–51

road signs, 47–48
Rome: contributions to modern alphabet, 76–77; copyists, 80–81; couriers and origins of postal system, 81–82; first daily newspaper, 81; Latin language, 75–77; public libraries, 80; writing, 77–80
Rosetta stone, 40–41

Sanskrit, 46

scrolls, 67–68, 71. *See* Dead Sea Scrolls
serifs, 77
Shih Huang Ti, 52–53
sign language, 60
Stone Age: cave paintings, 15–22; dating cave drawings, 17–18; early spoken communication, 13–15; engravings, 20–21; painting techniques, 19–20

talking sticks and cords, 62
telegraph system, Greek, 71–72
Ts'ai Lun, 49, 50

Vedic age, 45–46

wax tablets, 79
writing: on clay, 26–27; cuneiform, 27–28; demotic, 39; Greek, 66–67; hieratic, 39; Maya, 56–59; pictograms, 27–29, 38, 53; Roman, 77–80; on Rosetta stone, 40–41; writing materials in ancient Rome, 78–80

Note: There are alternate spellings for some of the names mentioned in this book. Here are three examples:
Confucius or K'ung-Fu-tzu (China)
Samarkand or Maracanda (China)
Erech or Uruk (Middle East)

About the Authors

Michael Woods is an award-winning science and medical writer with the Washington bureau of the *Toledo Blade* and the *Pittsburgh Post Gazette*. His articles and weekly health column, "The Medical Journal," appear in newspapers around the United States. Born in Dunkirk, New York, Mr. Woods developed a love for science and writing in childhood and studied both topics in school. His many awards include an honorary doctorate degree for helping to develop the profession of science writing. His previous work includes a children's book on Antarctica, where he has traveled on three expeditions.

Mary B. Woods is an elementary school librarian in the Fairfax County, Virginia, public school system. Born in New Rochelle, New York, Mrs. Woods studied history in college and later received a master's degree in library science. She is coauthor of a children's book on new discoveries about the ancient Maya civilization.

Photo Acknowledgments: The photographs in this book are reproduced courtesy of Giraudon/ Art Resource, NY, p. 1 (detail); DDB Stock Photo/© J.P. Courau, pp. 2-3; The Granger Collection, New York, pp. 11, 12-13, 16, 31, 37, 41, 47, 53; Gianni Dagli Orti/Corbis, pp. 21, 34-35; Scala/Art Resource, NY, p. 23; © Ronald Sheridan/ Ancient Art and Architecture Collection, pp. 24-25, 63; Allepo Museum Syria/The Art Archive, p. 28; Independent Picture Service, pp. 38 (all), 60; Bojan Brecelj /Corbis, p. 33; © ChinaStock, p. 43; Dinodia Picture Agency, pp. 44-45; ChinaStock/Wang Lu, p. 50; Werner Forman/Art Resource, NY, p. 55; DDB Stock Photo, pp. 56-57; Antochin Collection/The Art Archive, p. 59; Ashmolean Museum, Oxford UK/Bridgeman Art Library, 64; British Museum/The Art Archive, p. 69; British Library, p. 70; AKG London/ Gilles Mermet, p. 73; Museo Arceologico Nazionale, Naples, Italy/INDEX/Bridgeman Art Library, pp. 74-75 (detail); Archaeological Museum of Merida/The Art Archive, p. 76; St. Albans Museums, p. 79; NASA, p. 83.

Front cover: © British Museum/The Art Archive (left); © Bade Institute, Pacific School of Religion (right)

Cover background: Independent Picture Service